D0203944

*Lori discovers a healthy way to cope with a rainy day disappointment. Instead of negative behavior, Lori improvises an exciting dramatic story.*

# A Beach in My Bedroom

By Jane Belk Moncure

Illustrated by
Helen Endres

THE CHILD'S WORLD

ELGIN, ILLINOIS 60120

**Library of Congress Cataloging in Publication Data**

Moncure, Jane Belk.
  A beach in my bedroom.

  (Creative dramatics)
  SUMMARY: Disappointed because she cannot go to the beach, Lori imagines a beach in her bedroom.
  [1. Beaches—Fiction. 2. Play—Fiction] I. Endres, Helen. II. Title. III. Series.
PZ7.M739Be        [E]        77-12960
ISBN 0-89565-005-3

Distributed by Childrens Press, 1224 West Van Buren Street, Chicago, Illinois 60607.

# A Beach in My Bedroom

"I'm ready to go to the beach tomorrow," Lori told her mother. And she was. Her suitcase was packed.

She had her bathing suit,

her beach towel,

and her umbrella.

She had a sand pail,

a shovel,

and a big beach float.

She even had a fishing pole,

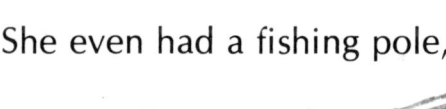

a basket of shells from last year,

and her elephant, Raja.

Lori put all of her beach things on the chair by her bed. She could hardly wait for tomorrow.

But during the night, there was a big storm. It was raining hard when Lori awoke.

"We can't go to the beach now," said Mother. "We will have to wait until the sun shines."

Lori was very sad! She sat on her bed and looked at all her beach things. Suddenly she had an idea.

"If I can't go to the beach, I will bring the beach into my bedroom," she said.

"Blue rug, I'll pretend you're my ocean."
And it was. Lori put on her bathing suit and
dived in for a swim. She splashed and kicked.

She jumped on her float.

"Bed," said Lori,
"I'll pretend you're my
sail boat." And it was.
  Lori hopped aboard
with Raja her elephant.

"The wind is blowing!" she called. "The boat is bumping up and down in the waves! Hold on!"

But Raja did not hold on. He fell into the ocean!

Lori had to rescue him.

"Poor Raja. You should learn how to swim," she said.

"Now, let's catch a big fish." Lori threw out her fishing line.

"Oh!" she cried. "I have hooked a giant shark! Help me pull him into the boat!"

Lori pulled and Raja pulled. . .but the shark got away.

"That's OK," said Lori. "I do not like sharks anyway. Let's run on the beach.

"Floor, you are my sandy beach," said Lori. And it was.

"I can hop," said Lori,

"and skip,

and do a flip!

I can roll over like an ocean wave,

walk sideways like a sand crab,

and pick up
all the shells
on the beach."

Then Lori put up her beach umbrella. "Now we will have a picnic," she said.

Lori found some dishes. She spread her beach towel on the sand.

"I will fix a banana sandwich for Raja," she said.

After the picnic, Lori and Raja went for a walk. "What do you think?" Lori asked Raja. "Could there be a treasure buried somewhere on this beach?"

"Toy box," said Lori, "you are the treasure chest. And pillows, you are the sand the treasure is buried under." And that's the way it was.

"The pirates buried their treasure chest way down deep in this sand," said Lori to Raja. "We will have to dig it out."

"It is out!" said Lori. She was about to open the treasure chest when there was a knock on her door.

"Lori," said Mother, "let's get ready. The sun is shining now. We are going to the beach."

And they did!

Creative dramatics provides a framework for the expression of many emotions and thoughts. Children are constantly dramatizing events that have happened to them, characters and situations they have seen on television, and happenings people have discussed with them. Through imaginative play, a child restructures his own experiences and discovers new ones. By imitating others in play, he comes to understand what they do and why, and also how their actions affect him.

**About the Author:**

Jane Belk Moncure, author of many books and stories for young children, is a graduate of Virginia Commonwealth University and Columbia University. She has taught nursery, kindergarten and primary children in Europe and America. Mrs. Moncure has taught early childhood education while serving on the faculties of Virginia Commonwealth University and the University of Richmond. She was the first president of the Virginia Association for Early Childhood Education and has been recognized widely for her services to young children. She is married to Dr. James A. Moncure, Vice President of Elon College, and currently lives in Burlington, North Carolina.

**About the Artist:**

Helen Endres is a commercial artist, designer and illustrator of children's books. She has lived and worked in the Chicago area since coming from her native Oklahoma in 1952. Graduated from Tulsa University with a BA, she received further training at Hallmark in Kansas City and from the Chicago Art Institute. Ms. Endres attributes much of her creative achievement to the advice and encouragement of her Chicago contemporaries and to the good humor and patience of the hundreds of young models who have posed for her.